Find Who You Are Meant To Be

Unleash Your Strengths, Become More Confident,

Transform Your Mindset, And Find Inner Peace

Steven Schuster

steveschusterbooks@gmail.com

Copyright © 2018 by Steven Schuster. All rights reserved.

No part of this publication may be reproduced, stored in a retrieval system, or transmitted in any form or by any means, electronic, mechanical, photocopying, recording, scanning or otherwise, except as permitted under Section 107 or 108 of the 1976 United States Copyright Act, without the prior written permission of the author.

Limit of Liability/ Disclaimer of Warranty: The author makes no representations or warranties with respect to the accuracy or completeness of the contents of this work and specifically disclaims all warranties, including without limitation warranties of fitness for a particular purpose. No warranty may be created or extended by sales or promotional materials. The advice and recipes contained herein may not be suitable for everyone. This work is sold with the understanding that the author is not engaged in rendering medical, legal or other professional advice or services. If professional assistance is required, the services of a competent professional person should be sought. The author shall not be liable for damages arising herefrom. The fact that an individual, organization of website is referred to in this work as a citation and/or potential source of further information does not mean that the author endorses the information the individual, organization to website may provide or recommendations they/it may make. Further, readers should be aware that Internet websites listed in this work might have changed or disappeared between when this work was written and when it is read.

For general information on the products and services or to obtain technical support, please contact the author.

Table of Contents

Introduction 9

Chapter 1: Knowing Thyself 15

Chapter 2: The Four Stages of Life 33

Chapter 3: Leave Your Old Self Behind 49

Chapter 4: Diversify Your Identity.................. 63

Chapter 5: It's Not About Who You Want to Be, But What You Are Willing to Sacrifice for It ... 77

Chapter 6: Restore Your Relationship with Failure 91

Chapter 7: Living in the Age of More 107

Chapter 8: Find Your "Purpose" 119

Chapter 9: Be Grateful for What You Have Now 129

Chapter 10: Lessons Learned: What Would I Tell My Teenaged, 20-, 30-, and 40-year-old Self? 139

Closing 153

Reference... 157

Endnotes 161

Introduction

They say life is a journey, not a destination. Liberal arts colleges and universities would certainly subscribe to this philosophy. No need to declare a major right away. Take your time and explore who you are and what you like as you get your education. Worry about making a plan later. My buddy Chris agreed whole-heartedly. If he could have spent five years backpacking through Europe, he would have, but his parents insisted he go to college right away. So he took the opportunity to enjoy the virtual smorgasbord of classes our liberal arts university had to offer.

He would start and stop taking classes with abandon. If he didn't like a professor, found the lectures boring, thought the workload was too challenging, or was receiving a grade his parents would not accept, he would drop the class within a few weeks. If a course caught his attention, seemed like an easy way to boost his credits, or was attended by a girl he liked, he was likely to enroll. He was on a six-year plan to earn a four-year bachelor's degree. Those of us who did not have wealthy parents paying for our entire collegiate experience and had to depend on scholarships, work study, and financial aid, shook our heads in bewilderment as we had to have a plan and take a much more direct path with our higher education.

He reminded me of those children whose parents sign them up for every sport and activity when they are very young just to see if there is one they might actually stick with. Finally, Chris had to face the real world when his parents realized that all of us who had entered school with him had already graduated and he still had yet to declare a major. It was then that I received a panicked call from him as his funding was about to expire and he still had no idea what he wanted to do with his life. We met, and I went through his college career with him class by class to see if we could cobble together some semblance of a field of study he was interested in and get him to a degree in the shortest amount of time.

He left that day with a plan, but I was still unconvinced that he would be successful as he really didn't seem committed to his path. I lost touch with Chris for a few years and didn't see him again until I returned to my alma mater for an alumni event. Much to my surprise, Chris was still there. Thankfully, it was not as a student. Rather, he was working in the admissions office recruiting prospective students and advising them on their collegiate experience. While I'll admit that at first glance it seemed a bit terrifying for Chris to give others advice on college choices, I soon realized that he was someone who these students could really relate to, as many of them were entering school unsure and overwhelmed. And Chris? He had finally found something he was passionate about. He loved our university, and he was eager to use the wisdom he had gained to mentor young adults so they could find out who they were a little sooner than he did. It was a good fit, and I couldn't have been happier for him.

Chris is not unique in his situation. He is certainly not alone in trying to discover who he is and what his purpose should be on this Earth. How well can anyone truly know a person?

How well do you know yourself? Have you already discovered everything there is to know? Are you aware of all of your goals, hopes, and talents? Do you feel like you have already achieved your full potential and are accomplishing everything you want to in life? Or do you consider yourself a work in progress? Are you content to learn more about yourself as you grow through your life experiences? Do you enjoy discovering new things about yourself along the way?

I had a plan in college and my professional life, and there are still days that I think to myself, "There's got to be something more." I love my life, and yet I wonder if I am on the path to fulfilling my potential and using my talents in ways that will truly make a difference in the world. I am sure you feel the same way.

Self-knowledge is a lifelong journey. We never completely know everything about ourselves — we are just gaining nuggets of insight along the way. The beauty is that there is always something new to discover. Imagine how sad it would be if there wasn't. There is always something more in store for us. There are always new challenges to overcome, new records to be broken, new discoveries to be made, and new ways to make a positive impact in our world. Life is a journey. There is much to do and the world is waiting, so let's get started on our path to knowing ourselves.

Chapter 1: Knowing Thyself

Our brains are infinitely inquisitive. They are constantly questioning things in order to gain new information. This is also true when it comes to ourselves. Even we are not off-limits when it comes to our human nature to question things. Wondering who we are, why we make the choices we make, and if we will ever be able to change are all ways we have likely questioned ourselves at one point or another in our lives. The answers we come up with are rarely permanent ones, but at least with each question, we gain more knowledge and insight into ourselves.

The desire to be knowledgeable about ourselves is not new. It is prevalent in most religions and philosophies throughout history. Psychological studies have found that the way we view ourselves has a tremendous impact on our lives. Our self-image affects everything from our behavior to the successes we experience.

When we believe that we are intelligent and good at solving problems, we behave in such a way that it becomes a self-fulfilling prophecy. We may be more likely to perform better on tests or in situations where those traits are valued. If we think we aren't good at public speaking, we will be more likely to carry ourselves in a defeated and nervous manner, which will prevent us from performing as well as we could if we believed in our abilities more.

Beliefs are powerful forces in our lives. Our healthy questioning of them serves to keep them in check. From an early age, my mother had convinced me that what I had to say mattered. She always took the time to listen to me, no matter how busy she was. When I was in elementary school, I discovered that I liked to write. My mother would not only hang my artwork and good grades up on the fridge, but she always praised and hung up my writing as well. She always told me that I had a gift for finding the right words, and that made me believe I was a writer from the time I was quite young.

My father was the first from his side of the family to attend college, and my siblings and I were the first generation of kids in the family who all attended college. When I got to college, I had an English professor who would always return my writing with a lot of red editing marks all over the page. It began to shake my belief in myself as a writer. I talked to my parents about it, and they told me one of two things could happen. Either I would change the way I thought of my writing completely and give up, thinking I was never really good at it, or I would see it as a challenge and a way to improve.

I decided to take option B. I went to my professor and asked him if he thought I had any potential to become a good writer, and if so, what he thought I needed to work on the most in order to improve. I'll admit, I was quite nervous to have that conversation, but

I will never forget his words. He said, "You are a lighthouse that acts as a beacon of light, shining brightly over a sea of mediocrity." He told me he didn't want me to see the quality of work being turned in by my peers and get complacent to do less than what we both knew I was capable of.

That experience in my collegiate career and his words helped to shape a belief in me that has had a great impact on my life. While I am in no way delusional enough to think that I am even close to being in the same league, I am sure that when Walt Disney was fired as an editor for not being imaginative and creative enough, or when Michael Jordan was cut from his basketball team, they used it to evaluate their beliefs in their gifts and talents, and let it inspire them to work even harder and fine tune their crafts. Beliefs are very powerful things indeed.

The tale of two brains

You know that your brain is always working — often beyond your immediate control and impossible to shut off. This may make the idea that you have two minds a daunting concept, but if you take the time to discover how your two minds work, you might find that you can use this to your advantage.

Please take a moment and close your eyes. Try to think of absolutely nothing. It's probably not as easy to do as you would think. Chances are you had thoughts sneak into your mind and you couldn't control them. This is the kind of mental chatter that constantly goes on in our brains, and it is extremely difficult to stop. If you have spent any time practicing or studying meditation, you will understand that these thoughts are the very things that people seek to quiet as they try to focus on being in the present. It doesn't come easily, and it takes some practice, for sure.

That is your thinking mind at work — the thoughts that are constantly parading through your mind and are often beyond your control. For me, this happens when I am in a meeting at work and my mind wanders to all the other things I need to be getting done. It happens when I bring work home, and all the while, I am thinking of how I should be spending time with my family. It happens when something made me angry or upset in the morning, and all day, thoughts of that event keep entering my mind as I get more and more worked up about it.

It even happens when I try to sleep at night and my brain can't stop thinking about things. I finally put a notebook and pencil on my nightstand. I found that I can fall asleep much faster if I jot down the ideas and thoughts that are keeping my mind so active. When I write them down, I no longer worry that I will forget them. It's a signal to my brain that I will address them tomorrow, and I can let them go in order to quiet my mind and get a more restful sleep.

Your thinking mind is also at work when you are up high and someone tells you, "Don't look down." What is the first thing you do? Look down, of course. You just can't help yourself. Or if someone tells you something negative that someone else said about you, the next thing out of their mouth is probably something like, "But don't worry about it. They don't know what they're talking about. Don't give it a second thought." Too late, right? Your thinking mind goes into overdrive, and it is all you can think about, which makes it nearly impossible to let go of.

Oh, the joys of the thinking mind… I'm sure you can think of infinite examples of when it has worked overtime in your life. The good news is that just by acknowledging all of those examples, you are demonstrating the work of your second mind: the observing mind.

Your observing mind is watching what your thinking mind is doing. While we can't actually control our thinking mind and get it to behave in the way we want it to, recall how we look down when we are told we shouldn't and can't get our minds off negative comments, even when we know that we should just let them go. Still, there are ways we can reframe our thinking and use it to our advantage. Just being conscious and aware of the activity in our thinking mind is a great place to start.

When we can acknowledge that our minds are not always under our control, we can begin to see that some of the beliefs we hold about who we are and what we are capable of may be incorrect. The purpose of this book is to help you discover who you are. The first step in knowing yourself is to recognize that sometimes your thinking can be unpredictable and unknown.

What to do with the unpredictable mind?

Our thinking mind and observing mind should be independent from one another as much as possible. It is important that our observing mind be able to recognize what our thinking mind is doing, so it needs to remain separate. The times when you have felt the most mental and emotional stress in your life is likely when the two minds were so interconnected that they seemed inseparable.

It is human nature to want to control your feelings — to get rid of the grief and sadness you feel over the loss of a loved one, or the anger and resentment you feel toward someone. The simple truth is that you can't. You can't control your thinking mind, and try as you might to stop them, these feelings will continue to sneak into your mind despite all of your best efforts to keep them out.

Emotions are not a choice, but behavior is.

Your feelings are what they are. You're not going to be able to change them. You feel what you feel. This may seem like a terrifying thought, but in reality, it is an empowering one. While it is true that you can't control your thinking mind, there is nothing that says you have to be controlled by it. You may not be able to control your feelings, but you are very much in control of the way you respond to them.

How can you deal with those strong emotions such as grief, anger, and fear that at times seem to dominate your life?

Recognize them, accept them, and make the conscious decision to move on in spite of them. Take your power back. Don't let your emotions define who you are. Acknowledge their existence. Accept that they are part of your life and will continue to enter your mind no matter what, but don't let them drive your life. Your feelings are not necessarily permanent, so don't resign yourself to thinking they have to be. Make the conscious choice to press on despite them.

Remember, you have two minds and you can only control one of them. Make the most of it. Don't let the thoughts and emotions you can't control determine who you are. Keep your identity, sense of self, and observing mind independent from your thinking mind and what goes on there. Admit that you are feeling grief, but not that you are sad. Acknowledge that you are feeling fear, but not that you are afraid. Just like Zen advises, say "I feel sorrow" instead of "I'm sad." Don't assimilate with your emotions. It seems like such a little thing, but it makes a huge difference in keeping thoughts and feelings as temporary residents in your brain.

What are your beliefs?

There are very few things in our world that everyone accepts as universal truths. It seems that everything is debatable. In a time when we have more data and information at our fingertips than ever before, you wouldn't think that this would be the case, but it is. Usually, at best, all we can hope for is a consensus that the majority of people will agree upon, but even that is often hard to come by. All data and information is viewed through the lens of the beholder. It is not only possible for people to look at the exact same information and reach entirely different conclusions, but it is almost certain.

Everything you believe about the world is a choice you have made at some point in your life. The choice may have been a deliberate and conscious one or a subconscious one, but you have decided to buy into all of your beliefs at one time or another. These beliefs are not always shaped by facts and evidence, but are often guided by emotion and impulse. In fact, sometimes we mold the facts and evidence to make it conform to and fit our beliefs. We may take incomplete memories and turn them into inaccurate ones by choosing to fill in the gaps with things we think must have been true that are supported by our beliefs. We all too often choose to see things the way we want to see them instead of as they really are.

Why can this pose a problem? There are two kinds of beliefs: those that help us and those that hurt us. In psychology, they refer to something called the confirmation bias. It is the natural tendency we have to only notice and pay attention to those things that support the beliefs we already have. It is not something we do intentionally. It is just human nature and how the brain is predisposed to deal with the massive amounts of information it receives. It is an unconscious bias we need to be aware of so we can overcome it and keep it from hurting us.

For example, if you grew up thinking you weren't very smart, you will always notice the mistakes you make and ignore all the times that people point out the smart things you do. If you think you are unattractive, you will focus on any negative reactions you get from others about your appearance and dismiss the positive ones.

All too often, the things about ourselves that we perceive to be problems or deficits are just unhelpful beliefs we have allowed to take hold. It doesn't matter whether a belief is true or not; what matters is whether it is helpful or harmful.

As we know, nearly everything is debatable and rarely accepted as universally true by everyone, so assess your beliefs. Look at them and evaluate them based on whether continuing to hold onto them is helpful to you. If they're not helpful, let them go.

Taking Responsibility

In this life, one thing is true: you are responsible for your own actions. Many things are beyond your control, but you hold the power to determine how your life will turn out. Yes, bad things will happen to you. It is not a matter of if, but when. Yes, they will feel awful, and will at times shake you to your core. But how you respond to them is up to you.

Your actions will decide whether you are going to be successful. You can choose to blame external factors and circumstances for your life, or you can choose to embrace the power you have and be the reason you get to celebrate your successes. You can't find out who you really are without accepting responsibility first.

Ralph Braun is an excellent example of someone who overcame some of the worst external circumstances you can imagine and surpassed everyone's expectations. He not only accepted responsibility for the quality of his life, but he also went on to tirelessly work to improve the lives of countless others. Braun said, "Rise above, my friends, and reach back to help others climb the ladder of life."

He was diagnosed with muscular dystrophy when he was six years old, and his parents were told not to expect for him to live to be a teenager. He became confined to a wheelchair at the age of 14, but he did not let this slow him down. When he was 15, Braun and his father created a motorized wagon to help him get around. Five years later, he created a motorized scooter that he called the Tri-Wheeler to help him ride to and from his full-time job. His employer moved farther away from his house, so Braun invented the Lift-a-Way wheelchair lift to enable him to get in and out of a van in his wheelchair. Soon others learned of his invention, and he created a business called Braun Corporation where these lifts, and ultimately other mobility assistive products under the name BraunAbility, were manufactured.

He was active in his company until he died in 2013 at the age of 72. He even went on to create the National Organization for Vehicle Accessibility to help those who could not afford the mobility products they needed to achieve their full potential in life.

Braun easily could have felt sorry for himself and helpless about the circumstances in his life. He could have given up and said everything was beyond his control, but he chose to accept responsibility for his own actions and successes in life instead. What a powerful example his life can be for the rest of us.

Key Takeaways:

- We have two minds: a thinking mind and an observing mind. The thinking mind is largely beyond our control, but the observing mind isn't. The two

should be independent from each other as much as possible.
- We can't control our feelings, but the way we respond to them is definitely within our power. We need to acknowledge and accept our feelings and thoughts for what they are, but work to keep them as temporary occurrences instead of permanent parts of our identity.
- Our beliefs are powerful thoughts that we have made a choice to buy into at some point. They are not always based on facts and evidence, and they are often guided by emotion and impulse.
- We should be willing to constantly question and reevaluate our beliefs. We need to ask ourselves if continuing to hold onto a belief is helpful or harmful. If a belief isn't helpful, we should let it go.
- We need to accept responsibility for our successes and disappointments instead of blaming external

circumstances when things don't turn out the way we hope. We can't control everything that happens to us, but we can absolutely control the way we respond to it. That is a big part of what defines who we really are.

Chapter 2: The Four Stages of Life

We all move through different stages of life as we grow and age. If we labeled these stages solely based on the age of a person, we might say that people progress through the stages of infancy, childhood, adolescence, adulthood, and old age. However, there are more to the stages of life that we will discuss in this chapter than just the number of years you have spent on Earth.

The idea of the stages of life is not new. The Hindu people have viewed their four stages of life as a crucial component of their societal and religious traditions since the 5th century B.C.E. They refer to their stages as *ashramas*. In a perfect world, every person would progress through all four stages, which are:

- Student: where they study and learn from experts to prepare themselves for their future career, family, and religious and societal expectations;
- Householder: where they get married and work to earn a living to support their family;
- Hermit (nearly nonexistent in today's Hindu society): when a person's children are grown and able to care for themselves, the older adults were expected to leave their home to live in a hut and give up most of their worldly possessions, as well as contact with most of their family, to spend time in reflective prayer;
- Wanderer: where they have given up all of their possessions, hopes, wishes, and responsibilities and spend time wandering at one with God until they die.[i]

Not all cultures are identical in the number of stages of life, their names for them, or the characteristics they assign to each stage, but many subscribe to the belief that people progress through various life stages. We will discuss the four stages of life common in our culture today.

Stage 1

A friend of mine was groomed to take over his family's bakery. He grew up watching his parents work and was assigned more responsibilities of his own in the bakery as he got older. After we graduated from high school, he made plans to attend culinary school in order to gain even more skills and hone his craft while he took business classes at night. He never gave a second thought to making plans of his own, because he knew his family expected him to take over the family business one day and it would make his parents proud. The problem was his heart wasn't in being a baker. He was a phenomenally talented artist, and would have preferred to spend his adolescence and early adulthood developing his artistic skills.

He finally had the difficult discussion with his parents. While they were disappointed at first that they would one day be selling their business instead of passing it along to their son, they acknowledged that their most important hopes and dreams had to do with him being happy in life. They happily supported him as his career aspirations took a very different path, but he had spent a lot of time trying to meet others' expectations and please them instead of focusing on his own goals and happiness.

This is the first stage of life to the letter. Stage 1 is the learning stage. It is when we observe and imitate others in an attempt to learn the skills and traits we will need throughout life. It sets the foundation for the future to come. By watching and mimicking others, we learn rules and socially accepted behaviors. We learn the way that others expect us to behave, think, and act. We are eager to fit in and please others, so we often do not think for ourselves and form our own independent set of values at this stage. [ii]

This stage often extends from infancy through adolescence and early adulthood, but everyone moves through the stage at their own pace and can easily become stuck, if they aren't careful.

Stage 2

A group of my high school buddies all went away to a big university together. Despite having different majors, they vowed to live together on campus and keep the gang intact. They shared stories of all of their new adventures with each other, but they experienced them separately. They attended different classes, were involved in different extracurricular activities, and made new friends. They started to find out that they had more in common with their new friends than with each other. They were finding out about themselves and were getting comfortable in their own skin. By the time the second semester rolled around, they had decided that they should try to change their housing arrangements. It wasn't that they didn't like and appreciate each other, but as they were coming into a new stage of life, they realized that their old high school friendships did not play as prominent a role as they had in the past. This fits in with Stage 2 of our lives, and is common for everyone.

Stage 2 is all about self-discovery, exploration, and being adventurous. It is about moving beyond trying to please others and meet their expectations, and instead asserting our independence and taking risks as we form our own understanding of the world around us. Stage 1 was all about fitting in, and Stage 2 is now about standing out — trying to discover and focus on what makes us different and unique. We no longer rely upon validation from others before we act and do not continue to put their opinions above our own. Their approval of our behavior is not as important to us during this stage (of course, there may always be certain people in our lives from whom we seek approval).

This is the stage where we meet new people, live in new places, and go through trial and error as we try to learn about ourselves. We discover our strengths and weaknesses, talents and difficulties, and begin to figure out what things in our lives are most important to us. This stage typically begins later in adolescence and lasts through our mid-20s to mid-30s, but again, everyone moves through the stage at their own pace and can get stuck for a longer period of time.

Stage 3

When my wife and I got married, we purchased a home of our own. Then it became a process of making our personal possessions, furniture, and décor come together in a harmonious fashion as we began to form our own little family unit. All of a sudden, my treasures from my bachelor days weren't as important to me as they once were. I found myself willing to part with things I never thought I would: my favorite couch, my broken-in recliner, and my t-shirt and jeans collection that had been such a big part of my life for so long suddenly didn't seem to fit with the man I had become. What was important was my bride and our happiness together. I was a different man now, and my priorities reflected that change. I was still close with my friends and we would make time to spend together, but by and large, my focus was on my career and family.

During Stage 3, we are gaining a better understanding of who we are than we have ever had before. We realize that we have a finite amount of time and energy in our day, and we don't want to waste that precious time on what isn't important to us. We stay in touch with the people who mean the most to us and are not interested in superficial relationships. We accept that we can't possibly be good at, or even try, everything in life, so we concentrate on the things we enjoy the most.

There are things we want to accomplish in our lives, and during this stage, we are laser-focused on making sure we do so. We reevaluate old dreams and goals and purge the ones that no longer work or hold meaning for us. Stage 3 is the one in which we realize what we are invested in and committed to. It usually happens from the time we are in our in our 30s until we retire, but it isn't the same for everyone.

Stage 4

When my grandmother was very ill and in the hospital for an extended period of time before she passed away, I visited her every day. On one of the walls of the hospital was a beautiful mural with a quote from a Greek proverb that said, "Society grows great when old men plant trees whose shade they know they shall never sit in." I would pass by that every day, and it gave me goosebumps each time as I always stopped and reflected upon it. I knew it was a reference to the many vibrant, active, wonderful older people who volunteered in the hospital, offering comfort to patients and families alike in their darkest hours. But I couldn't help but think of my grandmother too. While I was bringing in photo albums to help us share stories of happy times and wonderful family memories and trying to comfort and take care of her as she had done for me countless times, I thought of all the "trees" my grandmother had planted in me all throughout my life. Those "trees" were the nuggets of wisdom she shared with me, her unwavering belief in what she saw as my limitless potential, and the example she set for me through the way she lived her life. While she wouldn't be around to see the "trees" she planted in me reach full maturity, she tended to them anyway, making sure they took root and grew because she loved me and wanted nothing but the best for my life.

I will never forget all of the things my grandmother did to help make me who I am today. Even though she is no longer with me physically, she and the legacy she left behind live on through me, and I will make certain that they do in my children as well. This is a demonstration of the fourth stage of life at work.

In Stage 4, we begin to slow down a bit. We worked really hard in Stage 3 to make a difference in the world and build a legacy with our families and career. Stage 4 is now all about making sure that legacy lasts after we have passed away. It is the stage where we want to pass on our wisdom and values to younger generations so that we may live on in some way. We often choose to serve as mentors or volunteers during this stage. We are still very passionate about and committed to the things that mean so much in our lives, but we may no longer have the energy or ability to work for them in the same way that we did in Stage 3.

Getting Stuck

When people get stuck in a stage for a longer period of time than most, it is because they feel like they aren't good enough.

People who get stuck in Stage 1 don't like the things about themselves that make them unique. They try so hard to match the image that they believe others want them to be like, but try as they might, they feel like nothing they ever do is enough. The key is to realize that you will never to be able to please everyone, so it is best to just make decisions based on what is best for you.

When people get stuck in Stage 2, it is because they constantly feel like they need to be doing more, doing better, improving faster, achieving more, or living a more exciting and adventurous life. They also feel that despite their best efforts, whatever they do is never enough. It is important to recognize that it is impossible to do all that we'd like to in life, so focusing on what is most important is crucial.

In Stage 3, people get stuck when they fear that they haven't made enough of a difference in the world and they are committed to doing more. Again, they feel like what they do can never be enough. The key here is to understand that we all have limits to the amount of time and energy we are able to devote to things, so we need to be willing to help others begin to do the things we do.

It is even possible for people is Stage 4 to feel stuck if they are worried that their legacy will not live on to help future generations. They may think they have not done enough and want to cling to life in any way they can. It is key to recognize that change is something we can't avoid. [iii]

As we progress through the four stages of our lives, we are on a journey of self-discovery. We learn more about who we really are with each passing stage. It doesn't matter which stage we are currently in, or how long we are in there; we always have the opportunity to grow as a person and learn more about ourselves.

Key Takeaways

- Many cultures and religions have identified stages of life that people go through. They may differ in the names, the numbers, and the characteristics of each stage, but there are far more similarities than differences between them. These stages are a bit of a path to self-discovery as people learn about who they truly are along the way.
- Stage 1 is the learning stage where you observe and imitate others to try to fit in with the group, and where you learn the rules and expectations as well as socially acceptable behaviors. This is the foundation where you learn skills and behaviors you will need in the future.
- Stage 2 is the stage where you take more risks and assert some independence as you try to discover your own identity and sense of self. It is in this stage where you value your differences and start to form your own understanding of the world

around you. You explore new things through trial and error, and find your talents and weaknesses as you begin to figure out the things that really matter to you.
- Stage 3 is the stage where you realize that you have a limited amount of time and energy in your day, and you only want to spend it with the people and things that matter most to you. You figure out where you want your focus to be and you begin to "weed out" and separate from people and things that don't align with that. You reevaluate goals and friendships and begin to walk away from the ones that no longer serve your new purpose.
- Stage 4 is the stage when you try to make sure that the legacy you will leave behind will live on in future generations. You pass on your wisdom and values to members of your family, or your community

through volunteering and mentoring others.

Chapter 3: Leave Your Old Self Behind

Sometimes we make mistakes to identify who we are — even if we think we know.

We like to think of ourselves as rational people who are perfectly capable of judging situations, others, and ourselves fairly and objectively. Most times, this is simply not the case. It isn't intentional, and it isn't even usually our fault, but it is how our brains are wired, and we need to be aware of it in order to overcome it.

Our brains take in unbelievably large amounts of information. In order to help process and sort through all of this information, the brain comes equipped with many biases. While this is helpful to the brain, it isn't always helpful to us, because it often gives us an inaccurate picture of reality that distorts our views as we attempt to make informed decisions.

One of these biases is the Actor Observer Bias. This is where we judge a situation and the participants very differently depending on the lens we are viewing it through.

For example, when it is my turn to pick up things at the grocery store, it isn't usually a pleasant experience. I get very annoyed when people push their carts out in front of me, cutting me off without looking, and when they stand in the middle of the aisles having conversations, it makes it difficult for the rest of us to get around them. When these things happen, I feel myself seething, dumbfounded by how rude and inconsiderate people can be as they think their time is more valuable than mine and try to push their way through the store.

On the "rare" occasions when I might push my cart out of an aisle, cutting someone off, I view it as an innocent mistake and something the other person surely shouldn't be upset by.

When I run into someone I know and we talk for a few minutes in the middle of the aisle, I view it as harmless, because after all, the people can get around us if they need to. What a different perspective I have on the very same situation when I am the guilty party instead of someone else. I judge others very harshly and consider them to be ill-mannered, rude, and inconsiderate, while I think of myself as having good intentions and just making a simple mistake.

Clearly, the moral of my story is that I should no longer go grocery shopping, or that we can't just accept our judgment of ourselves at face value. We often make mistakes as we try to evaluate ourselves.

We think we know what makes us happy and what makes us miserable, but it turns out that even our perception of that is often distorted. When we don't land the promotion or great job we really want, we feel terrible, but in reality, the sun will come out again tomorrow and it isn't the end of the world. It turns out that when we remember the situation in the future, we will remember it as being even worse than it really was. When we think of the new job or big promotion and what it would have meant for our life, we overestimate how happy it would make us. Our mind is constantly playing tricks on us and altering our views of reality.

Another bias that our brains tend to rely on is the confirmation bias. This is where we only use logic and reasoning to support the beliefs we already have. This can result in us thinking we know things that in reality we do not know for certain, or in us knowing something but thinking that we don't.

For example, my wife is a brilliant woman who knows me very well, but even she is susceptible to making errors in her judgment of me from time to time. I was recently late getting home for dinner, and when I arrived, the look on her face let me know that she was not pleased. She automatically thought she knew why I was late — that I had gotten tied up with my work and lost track of time.

Since this may have happened a time or two in the past, she used logic and reasoning to confirm a belief that she already had about me. I sometimes get wrapped up in what I am doing at work and do not pay attention to the time. While this is true, it was not the case that time.

I knew she had had a rough week at work and I wanted to do something nice for her, so I stopped at the florist to pick her up a bouquet, and that had caused me to be late for dinner. My wife thought she knew what had happened, but she really did not.

Our emotions, or even the unconscious memory of them, can have a tremendous effect on the way we view people and situations, as well as the decisions we make. This is often not to our benefit, because they can definitely cloud our judgment and cause us to make rash irrational decisions. When I was 20, I was holding my grandmother's hand, sitting beside her hospital bed when she received the devastating diagnosis that she had stage four terminal cancer and that she likely only had a few months to live, as there was no treatment they could give her. My grandmother and I were very close (as you can see by now), and I was heartbroken, as I knew the doctor's words would change my family's lives forever. To this day, I absolutely hate hospitals and going to the doctor, even for a checkup, because I have forever linked the experience I had with my grandmother many years ago and the emotions that came with it to the entire medical profession.

The logical side of me knows that I am being irrational and that going to the doctor is smart, and can ultimately save many lives through preventative medicine, but the emotional side of me is absolutely terrified of getting bad news anytime I or anyone I love has to go to the doctor or hospital. My blood pressure and pulse always read as elevated in the doctor's office because I am so nervous, and they always take it multiple times when I am there. I even hate to take my pets to the vet because they are like family members too. I know it doesn't make any logical sense, but my emotions still overrule that logic to this day.

We aren't always who we think we are. As we have discussed, our brains can play tricks on us in ways that may make us believe certain things about ourselves that aren't always true. On top of that, there are many different facets to our identities.

We behave in one way at work and another way at home. The way we speak with our friends is not the same way we would speak around our parents. So how do we know our true selves? The things that happen in our lives mold and shape our perceptions, goals, values, and identities. It is not necessary to think of our identities as static and unchanging. This often makes us confine ourselves to the preconceived notions we have about ourselves, instead of encouraging us to think of ourselves as works in progress capable of growth and change. It is important to learn as much as we can about ourselves, but we should never stop examining who we are. There is a distinct possibility that something may occur in our lives that will mean who we are today will not be exactly the same as who we are tomorrow.

"To become a new version of yourself, you have to let go of your old self — and old struggles and hurts."

We change. That is a certainty on which we can rely. We will not stay the exact same person all throughout our lives. We are meant to grow and change — not to remain static.

Change is a form of loss. I know we are all experts when it comes to feeling loss, and change is certainly not the first word that comes to our minds when we think of loss. We think about all of the terrible sadness we have felt from losing loved ones who have passed away, or from the painful breakups we have endured in our past relationships. We may even think of times that we have lost money or a job we loved, but we probably do not think of change as a loss when in fact, it is.

A loss is when we no longer get to be around a person or thing that meant so much to us, and we will never experience that relationship or thing in exactly the same way again. The same is true about change. Once we change, we never experience life in exactly the same way we did before. Whoever you were in the past is gone. You can't be that person forever because you change and improve. If you have pain from your past, try to let go of it first and then close the door on it and move on. The person you were in the past doesn't need to be present in your future.

As we grow and move through the stages of our lives, we change. This is largely because our sense of self and identity are impacted greatly by the meaning we get from the relationships in our lives. As we progress through the four stages of life, our priorities change, and we discover more about ourselves. As we do, we constantly reevaluate how we spend our time and who we spend it with. We decide to give some relationships less importance in our lives or end them altogether. This can create a feeling of emptiness until we slowly replace those relationships with new ones. All of this helps to change our identity. While this isn't necessarily a bad thing, we still experience change as a loss (at least until we regain our footing afterward).

Solution to loss

The first step is to recognize that our memories are selective. They often make us think that things in the past were perfect, even when they weren't. It is human nature to only remember the best parts of our pasts, which makes us nostalgic for them once they are gone. We become convinced that our lives would be so much better if we could just return to the time before our loss.

The second step is spend as much time as possible with the people who care about, know, and love you unconditionally. It's hard work to regroup and recover after you suffer a loss of any kind. Allow them the opportunity to help and support you.

The third step is to take time for yourself. Allow yourself to feel what you feel without beating yourself up for it. Then start taking care of yourself — physically, mentally, and emotionally. Go outside to enjoy some sunshine and fresh air. Eat, sleep, and exercise better. Do some things just for you that you've been putting off because you've been too busy. Take a break from the stressful things in your life to do something just for the pure joy of doing it.

Losses are a fact of life. They are unavoidable. We suffer unimaginably painful losses of those we love when they pass away. We lose friendships, relationships, jobs, and money. We lose old hopes, dreams, and beliefs that no longer serve our purpose in life.

We lose parts of ourselves as we close a chapter in our lives and change our identity and sense of self. Losses are a natural part of our ability to grow and change. Losses and growth go hand in hand. It is impossible to have one without the other. Growing is all about taking a moment to be sad and nostalgic about the parts of us we leave behind while being proud of what we've accomplished and embracing the new person we have become. We need to acknowledge and accept our losses, make peace with them, and then begin moving forward so we can discover the best version of our future selves.

Don't forget that eventually, everything will be lost. Even your life. So embrace the life of today and breathe, my friend.

Key Takeaways

- Even when we think we know who we really are, chances are we have made some mistakes and incorrect assumptions about ourselves. Our brains can play tricks on us, and our biases can get in the way of giving us a fair and accurate picture of our true selves.

- We should not view our identities as static and unchanging, but rather as works in progress perfectly capable of growing and evolving over time.
- Change is a certainty guaranteed to happen throughout our lives. Change is also a form of loss, because once we change, we will never experience our lives in exactly the same way again.
- We need to acknowledge the loss we feel and then forge ahead to create our new sense of self, leaving our old self and the pain behind.
- Loss is inevitable, and growth and loss go hand in hand. It is impossible to have true growth without some loss in which you leave a part of your old self behind. It is important to make peace with the loss and then work to leave it behind so you can move forward and discover your best self.

Chapter 4: Diversify Your Identity

"Don't put your eggs all in one basket" are wise words from a proverb that my mom told me on many occasions during my childhood and adolescence. It was her way of shielding me from disappointment, as she knew that if I put all my hopes, dreams, and efforts into only one area of my life, disappointment would be sure to follow. I heed her words even today in so many areas of my life. I will share a few examples with you.

The Stories

Twice a year, I trudge into my bank to have the obligatory meeting with my investment advisor. I trudge because admittedly, I know as little as possible about my 401K and the stock market. I only know enough to worry when I see the red downturned arrows on the news and see that the value of my overall portfolio has dropped. My advisor reminds me not to worry in the short-term because my investment is a long-term one for my retirement.

He tells me that I have a diversified portfolio, which means it is spread out across many different types of companies, and that is done to keep my investments from becoming too risky. If one type of company I am invested in loses value, chances are good that another type of company in my portfolio will do well and balance it out so that I don't suffer a major loss. I tell him my mom would be pleased that I don't have all of my eggs in one basket. Then he chuckles and says that is exactly right. This is the dance we do with each other every six months to ease my mind and earn his paycheck.

Besides diversifying your finances, diversifying your life and identity can come in handy as well, especially if things don't turn out the way you hope. One of my best friends in high school was a very talented volleyball player who planned to continue to play in college. In fact, she was offered a full athletic scholarship — until she injured her knee so badly halfway through her senior season that her doctor told her if she wanted to be able to walk when she was 30, playing volleyball was no longer an option for her. She was devastated, but fortunately for her, her parents had insisted that she develop a well-rounded resume filled with much more than just her athletic talent. It included earning straight As, being involved in numerous clubs and activities, and performing a great deal of community service. While she decided to turn down her offer of an athletic scholarship, she was still contacted by 232 colleges and universities in 38 states who tried to convince her to attend their school. She earned many scholarships which paid her tuition in full. Talk about a tangible way that diversifying her identity and activities really paid off, and helped her to overcome some very challenging circumstances!

In 2009, the *Harvard Business Review* published an article discussing the staggering and alarming increase in work-related suicides. It identified a company, France Telecom, in which 24 employees had committed suicide in the span of a year with even more employees making unsuccessful attempts. This is not isolated to one specific company or country, though. Sadly, these tragedies are occurring more all around the world. America's Bureau of Labor Statistics reported that work-related suicides in the United States increased 28% from 2007 to 2008. It seems that in an increasingly competitive global economy where employees are expected to deliver greater results in less time with fewer resources, more and more of them are collapsing under the pressure. For people who base their identity and sense of self almost entirely upon their work performance, this can prove to be too much for them to handle. [iv]

When I was in high school, a member of our wrestling team suffered an unimaginable loss when his father committed suicide. I will never forget seeing him and his mother walking out of the guidance office, sobbing uncontrollably like their whole world had been ripped away from them. I wasn't sure why they were so inconsolable at the time, but I came to find out later that day that his father had walked out of his office at work in the middle of the day, driven straight home, left a note for his family, and then proceeded to shoot himself while sitting at his desk.

The note he left behind apologized to his wife and three sons for failing as the provider for their family. He had not met the quota at work that he needed to in order to earn his large salary bonus, and he feared that he would be unable to meet their financial obligations. He believed the only way that his family would be financially secure again is if they used his life insurance money to pay off their debts.

While his wife and sons mourned the loss of their cherished loved one, they were thinking of the fun times they had shared together when he wasn't working, and all of the times he had made them feel better when they were hurt or sick. They thought of all of the holidays and birthdays they spent together and how he attended their sporting events when he could to cheer them on. They remembered a beloved father and husband while, tragically, he only thought of himself as a provider. When that seemed to go horribly wrong, the depression and disappointment he felt was too much to bear, as his entire identity seemed tied to his ability to provide for his family financially. That is where he found the value in himself.

What is identity?

Identity is the idea we have about who we are and how we relate to those around us. It is how we would describe ourselves to someone who asked us to tell them a little about ourselves. It is how we define ourselves and view our place in the world. The way we identify ourselves might include our position in our family, profession, gender, race, religion, ethnicity, citizenship, and many other possible descriptors. Generally speaking, our identity and sense of self usually comes from the parts of ourselves that we are the most proud of and that we feel sets us apart from everyone else. They usually make us feel good and give us a healthy sense of self-esteem.

The identities we assign to ourselves usually fall into one of three categories:

- Role Identities are the labels we give ourselves based on duties we are expected to perform, specific responsibilities we have, or the place we hold in our families. Examples include mother, father, son, daughter, teacher, doctor, lawyer, truck driver, student, etc.

- Type Identities are the labels given to people who are thought to share things in common like physical appearance, behavior, opinions, values, location and/or historical connection, etc., even when it is believed that these shared characteristics may only last for a set period of time: Examples include toddlers, teenagers, Americans, Italians, Kenyans, South Koreans, Democrats, Republicans, African-Americans, Hispanics or Latinos, heterosexuals, homosexuals, bisexuals, etc.

- Personal Identity includes any other description that people would assign to themselves that they consider to be a truly integral part of who they are. It might be the color of their hair, their style of dress, their religion, their unusual height, their town, their membership in a club or organization, attitudes, values, or anything else they would like to share with others when they introduce themselves. [v]

Our identity and sense of self usually comes from the things we appreciate most about ourselves. It is unique to everyone, but is typically derived from us examining what sets us apart from society as a whole and how we measure up to and compare with others. It might involve our career success, education level, income, athletic or academic ability, religion, popularity, physical attractiveness, support of a sports team, or a variety of other possibilities. Often, a large part of what we choose to include in our identity is set in our youth, as we value the things about ourselves that we receive praise and attention for when we are young. Unfortunately, we sometimes suffer a traumatic experience in our youth that becomes permanently embedded in the way we see ourselves, such as surviving abuse or a critical illness, or the loss of a parent or very close loved one.

The solutions to diversify your life

The first thing you need to do is assess where you are putting your focus, time, and energy in your life. The parts of your life to which you are directing most of your attention are the ones you are making a priority and are serving as the biggest influences on your identity.

Self-questioning is a powerful tool when you want to discover what your dominant identity type is at the current moment. What defines you the most? Your job? Your partner? Your hobby? You being American? Or gay? Or Asian? What is the identity type that leaves the greatest mark on you — positively or negatively?

Ask yourself which areas of your life you feel the most protective over and which ones terrify you when you think of the possibility of failing in them. Ask yourself who you are if they take away your work. If you can expand your time and attention beyond your relationships and work, then you are well on your way to diversifying your identity.

When you choose an area of your life that you'd like to give more attention to, commit to it. It is only when you spend time doing something repeatedly that it becomes part of your identity.

Have goals in all areas of your life, some target that you can still shoot at if you get fostered of other aims. That will help to ensure that each part of your life receives some of your attention, and that you have something to work toward and improve. [vi]

Key Takeaways

- Don't put all of your eggs in one basket. Diversifying your identity is important. It can protect you from extreme disappointment if something should go wrong in your life. You will still be able to rely on the other areas of your life to help see you through the difficult times.

- Our identity is the idea we have about who we are and how we relate to the people around us. It is the way we view our place in the world.
- The way we identify ourselves might include our position in our family, profession, gender, race, religion, ethnicity, citizenship, and many other possible descriptors.
- Our identity may be shaped by the things we received praise and attention for in our youth, or by enduring a traumatic event.
- In order to diversify your life, you must first evaluate where you are spending most of your time, focus, and energy. Commit to spending time regularly in a new or underappreciated area of your life in order to make it a more prevalent part of your identity.

Set goals in all areas of your life so your can strive toward improvement.

Chapter 5: It's Not About Who You Want to Be, But What You Are Willing to Sacrifice for It

On January first each year, like clockwork, the majority of Americans reflect upon their lives and set goals for the upcoming year. I had a hunch that I knew what the most common New Year's resolutions were so I did a little research to test my theory. It turns out that I was correct. On every single poll that asked people to share their resolutions, losing weight and exercising more were always among the top four resolutions people made.

These are noble resolutions, because exercising more and losing weight can have tremendous health benefits for everyone. The problem with these two resolutions is that they are labor-intensive. They require effort, commitment, and follow-through, or they are nothing more than wishes.

It is not enough to want to lose weight and exercise more — you have to be willing to put in the work and make the sacrifices necessary to make it happen. That means sacrificing by getting up at 5:00 a.m., if necessary, to get your workout in rather than hitting the snooze button and staying in bed. It means sacrificing by running in the cold, heat, or rain. It means sacrificing by exercising when you are sore, tired, busy, or when it is simply the last thing you want to do. It means sacrificing by spending money on a variety of fresh fruit and vegetables, taking the time to research healthy recipes, and learning to prepare meals in a different way.

Without consistent hard work and sacrifice, these resolutions don't stand a chance of being achieved.

How much pain are you willing to take, and for what?

What do you want out of life? If you are like most people, you probably responded with things like happiness, a close family, a career you enjoy, financial stability, and good health. While these things are all wonderful, they are just wishes without action. Asking what you want out of life is not a great way to predict whether you will be successful. Everyone can answer that question pretty easily.

If I asked you instead, "What you are willing to struggle for in your life?" or "What pain would you be willing to endure in order to achieve your goals?" you may need to think about that a little more.

That would require more of a commitment and sacrifice from you, and your answer would probably make me better able to determine whether or not I think you are likely to be successful. It would give me a better idea of the value you place on your goals.

Everyone wants the amazing things in their lives, but not everyone is willing to go through the struggles and put in the work required to make their goals and dreams a reality.

The good times are easy. Everyone can handle those. It's in the difficult times that we see what you are made of. Knowing if you will be able and willing to endure the negative things in order to eventually get to the good on the other side is a much better predictor of whether you will be successful in life. If you are good at handling the negative experiences that come your way, then you will experience success in your life.

If you truly want something, you will be willing to roll up your sleeves and work for it until you make it happen. If you find that you are content to sit back and wish and hope for something you want for a long period of time, you may want to reevaluate that goal, because it might not really be a priority for you. You might not want it as badly as you think you do. Making this realization and stepping back from such a goal won't make you a loser or a quitter. It is a sensible thing to disengage your energies from something unproductive and regroup your strengths and focus to serve a goal that you're more committed to.

Your life isn't all going to be sunshine and roses. That is a fact. Asking you what you want from life is a bit like sending you through an all-you-can-eat buffet. You can go along and pick anything you want without having to make any commitments yourself. That is entirely too easy and quite unrealistic. By being asked what sacrifices you are willing to make and what pain you are willing to endure, you are forced to think and start making some more difficult choices. Your answer is what sets you apart from everyone else and makes you who you are.

If you walk into any elementary classroom and ask the boys what they want to be when they grow up, you are likely to find several who tell you they want to be a professional football player. They will be able to tell you how excited they are to chase that dream and exactly which players they are hoping to be like. Some of them will continue to believe in that dream as they play on their high school and college teams, but most will abandon that dream and pick a new career path before they ever even attempt to impress professional team scouts. Why is that? Are they all quitters? Are they afraid of failure? Did they stop believing in themselves?

Not at all. They may have been interested in the results of being a professional football player: big contracts, accolades, adoring fans, fame, fortune, etc. What they may not have been interested in was all of the conditioning in the off-season, weight training, lifestyle changes, criticism from coaches, injuries, and *work* it would take to achieve that dream. They may simply have decided that the sacrifices they would have to make were not worth the rewards. They may just have decided they didn't want to become a professional football player as much as they had previously thought (or at all). They made some discoveries about themselves and then reevaluated their goals. They got rid of one that no longer made sense or was a priority for them.

Your future will be defined by the goals, values, and beliefs you are willing to fight for. It is your struggles that will determine where you find success in life. You can say you want anything in the world, but until you prove it by putting in the hard work, it simply isn't true.

Actions speak louder than words.

What pain is worth sustaining?

Anything you deem worth having should mean that you are willing to commit to the struggles you will need to go through in order to make it happen. The things you decide are important to you and priorities in your life should inspire you to work harder and struggle more to achieve them than you would be willing to for the other things in your life. That is the kind of pain that is worth sustaining — the kind that keeps you moving ever closer to reaching your goals and causes you to grow and change.

This pain does not go away overnight, though it is temporary. However, if you quit everything before you earnestly start and are never willing to put in any work to achieve your goals or become your best self, that pain will last forever, as you will always find yourself wondering what might have been.

When we decide whether a goal is worth our time, effort, and energy, we should compare the pain necessary to pursue the goal to the pain of not working toward the goal. This will allow us to decide which is the pain we are willing to sustain. Let me give you a few examples. If you are contemplating whether exercising to lose weight is something you want to commit to, you might ask yourself if you are willing to sustain the pain of sore muscles and consistent early morning workouts in order to work toward the new goal, or if you are willing to tolerate the pain of increased risk of heart disease and diabetes and being unable to match the energy of your children if you decide to maintain your current lifestyle choices.

If you are contemplating relocating for a new job, you will need to decide if you are willing to sustain the pain of moving away from family and friends, as well as the fear and loneliness that may accompany being in a new place as you build your reputation from the ground up in a new position, or if you would rather tolerate the pain of staying in your current job, which may not offer you any new challenges or opportunities for advancement, and which you no longer find enjoyable or rewarding. Thinking of decisions in this way may offer you a whole new perspective to consider.

I have made some choices about the pain I am willing to endure so far in 2018 as I try to discover more about myself and ultimately become the best version of myself that I can. I will share a few with you:

- I am willing to endure the pain of not bringing work home with me at least three days per week. This drives me crazy because I feel like I am falling behind, but I have decided the struggle is worth it because I value spending quality time with my family more.
- I am willing to endure the pain of giving up some of my free time on Saturdays to volunteer in my community. This is important to me because I want to be a role model for my kids.
- I am willing to endure the pain of the sometimes less-than-pleasant sounds of children practicing musical instruments, as well as the cost of purchasing instruments and paying for lessons, because I want my children to have the freedom to explore new things and become well-rounded individuals.

If you realize you are not willing to pay the "pain price" for something, it is time to change.

James J. Mapes in his book *Quantum Leap Thinking: An Owner's Guide to the Mind* offers some good insight into the way change works in our lives. Change usually occurs for one of three reasons:

- we suffer from some sort of tragedy or traumatic event like the death of a loved one, surviving a natural disaster, losing a job, getting a divorce, or having a serious illness;
- we have avoided change for so long that everyone else changed around us, and we no longer have any other choice except to change;
- we change deliberately because we want to improve and create a better future for ourselves.

Change goes through three stages. First, we have to be willing to let go of the past. Then we go through a period of adjustment and confusion where we are nostalgic about what we gave up and wonder if we made the right choice, while we are at the same time hopeful about the good things that may arise from us making a change. Finally, we fully accept the change and work to become comfortable with it and incorporate it into our lives. [vii]

If you decide that something in your life is causing you pain and struggles that you are no longer willing to tolerate, or that it is simply no longer serving your identity and purpose well, this is all part of your self-discovery journey, and it should be embraced. You can make a plan to change the things that aren't working for you anymore. There are several things to keep in mind:

- Meaningful long-term change does not happen overnight. There will be successes and setbacks. Things will not always be easy. You will need to take the good with the bad while you try to persevere and keep moving forward to your goal.

- Break the change down into small, manageable steps so that you are not overwhelmed and tempted to give up.
- Make a plan for yourself and set mini-goals and deadlines. It should help to keep you focused, on track, and moving forward, and allow you to celebrate even small successes along the way. This can help you stay motivated, even when difficulties arise.
- Be patient with yourself and try not to get discouraged if the change is not happening as smoothly and quickly as you had hoped. Be ready to lean on those closest to you for support, if need be.

Key Takeaways

- Consistent hard work and sacrifice are a necessary part of any worthwhile and meaningful change.

- You need to decide how much pain and struggle you are willing to endure in order to achieve your goals.
- It is the struggles and difficult times you persevere through which will determine the successes in your life.
- If you decide something in your life is no longer worth enduring the pain and struggle for, it is time to make a change.
- Recognize that meaningful long-term change does not happen overnight, and it is not easy. You will need to accept the successes and setbacks in order to persevere and achieve your desired outcome.

Chapter 6: Restore Your Relationship with Failure

Okay, I'll own up to it: I am one of the people who did not pass his driving test on the first try. The examiner let me know that I had hit an orange cone while trying to parallel park during the exam. Apparently, since that cone represented either a pedestrian or a car, that was a big no-no and kept me from earning a passing score. As much as I hated getting the bad news that I had failed, at least by knowing where I went wrong, I knew what to target in my marathon practicing sessions before I took the test again. I am pleased to say my second attempt was a success, and I have been happily driving ever since.

I chose to own my failure and use the knowledge I gained from it to drive me toward success in the future. People often have very different reactions to failure. The four different relationships people typically have with failure are:

- Oblivion (they don't know what they don't know): These people don't recognize that they are actively avoiding participating in things due to their bad relationship with failure. They come up with all kinds of reasons why they don't do things, why they don't go out on a limb and live their life to the fullest. All the while, they never realize what is preventing them from reaching their goals and living their best life is their fear of failure. They have a subconscious fear that others will judge them, or that they will be humiliated if they aren't successful at something, so they don't even try.

- Self-chosen Oblivion (they know that they don't know): These people are aware that they have a fear of failure, and they don't invest themselves in activities in a conscious effort to protect themselves. They have decided that it's best, and safer, not to even try new experiences because failure is not a feeling they want to know. They realize that there is something missing from their life and that it is not as vibrant and full as it could be, but their fear of the failure prevents them from becoming engaged. Instead, they often choose to live vicariously through others and "take their word for it," rather than experiencing things firsthand.

- Oblivion against Experience (they don't know that they know): These are the people who live in a state of perpetual denial. It is said that the definition of insanity is doing the same thing over and over and expecting a different result. That is exactly how these people operate. These are the people who are doomed to repeat history because they refuse to learn from it. They have experienced failure at times, but instead of learning lessons from the failure and the mistakes they have made, they dismiss them as flukes or explain them away as being perfectly normal occurrences that everyone experiences. Then they keep doing the same things they have always done before.

- No Oblivion (they know that they know): These people have experienced failure, and they are not afraid of experiencing it again. They know that whatever fear they may had of failing, things never turned out as bad as they imagined they would. They learn lessons from failure and use that new knowledge to help them do better in the future. They know that failure is a natural part of life and trying to avoid it will only serve to prevent them from living their life to the fullest. They are determined not to let that happen.

People are all too often unaware of their relationship with failure. They hold back from fully participating in life all because of a fear of failure. This stands in the way of their self-discovery and growth and keeps them from living their best life.

Why do people fail?

There are numerous reasons why people fail. We will discuss some of them here.

People are afraid to stand out and be different from everyone else.

It can be terrifying to draw attention to yourself and be brave enough to stand out from the crowd. Our comfort zone is to blend in with everyone else. Achieving our full potential often requires us to set ourselves apart. As I experienced as a former high-school student and teacher, students seem to be much more comfortable blending in with their buddies. In class, many don't want to raise their hands to answer too many questions. They don't want to draw attention to the fact that they are earning good grades. They seem to be perfectly content to be just like everyone else.

I used to be like this too, as a kid. Then I realized that in order to keep my buddies from feeling bad about themselves, I was settling for being average. I knew if I wanted to earn scholarships and go after my dreams, I was going to have to step up and do more, and I didn't need to apologize to others for that.

People give up too soon.

We live in a society where instant gratification is valued so much that we are all too often unwilling to wait for the payoff over the long haul. Think of how many great inventions would never have been created if people had thrown in the towel after the first time they failed. Many famous people wouldn't have achieved their personal greatness if they gave up. Michael Jordan got cut from his high school basketball team, and look where he ended up — all because he was willing to put in the work and persevere.

People assume they know everything.

The most successful people in life are often those who are humble enough to admit they don't have all of the answers and are willing to seek the advice and counsel of people who do. Being willing to learn from others is a sign of strength — not weakness.

People don't take responsibility for what happens in their lives.

Too many of us are all too willing to give our power away. We are content to view ourselves as victims to which bad things happen, rather than powerful individuals ready to roll up our sleeves and get to work.

When we fail, many of us are happy to blame everyone and everything else, instead of thinking: *So things didn't work out — now what can I do to improve for the future?*

People take their eye off the prize.

It is rather scary how short the human attention span is. It is human nature to be distracted by other things. Truly successful people can maintain their focus on their goals and not get distracted by emails, social media, other people's opinions, or just life in general.

People fail to plan.

If you don't know where you're going, how will you ever know when you get there? People who don't have a plan are easily sidetracked by anything new that comes along and rarely reach their goals. "Failing to plan is planning to fail," after all.

People have a fear of failure.

People who are afraid to fail are happy to maintain the status quo, but are unwilling to move forward in a way that will help them live their life to the fullest and reach their true potential. They become stuck in quicksand and are paralyzed, unable to propel themselves toward their goals.

People want to achieve every success immediately.

Often, when people find out that achieving their goals is going to be harder than they thought and will require more work on their part than they expected, they can be overwhelmed and want to give up.

People don't believe in themselves.

There will be challenges and difficulties in life. That is inevitable. Truly successful people believe that they have the ability to find the solutions necessary to overcome whatever challenges arise.

People don't take the time and effort to learn from past mistakes.

While it is human nature to want to put mistakes and failures out of our minds as quickly as possible, that is not always in our best interest. It is equally unhelpful to dwell too long in the negative and be unable to move on, but taking some time to learn from our mistakes will pay off in spades. It is important to find the right balance.

How to handle failure

Getting to the real root of why we are afraid to fail can go a long way toward helping us overcome that fear and begin moving toward our goals. We often stop at the superficial answers when we question what we are afraid of failing at. We may think we are afraid of losing money or tarnishing our reputation, but in reality, our fears often run much deeper than that.

Many times, the fears holding us back can be traced back to values engrained in us in our childhood. Maybe we were taught to be grateful for what we had and were discouraged from wanting more. Maybe we were taught that we should always be humble and not try to set ourselves apart from others. Maybe we were taught to value security and stability above all else.

While these values are not bad ones to have, sometimes we can take them to the extreme and allow them to prevent us from taking chances and trying new experiences. We need to practice them in the right balance and reassure ourselves that it is okay to move toward our goals at a pace that is comfortable for us.

Derek Sivers, former musician, producer, circus performer, entrepreneur, and TED speaker in his article *Think Like a Bronze Medalist, Not Silver*, points out that our happiness depends in large part on where we place our focus. He encourages us to avoid thinking like a silver medalist — being unhappy and disappointed because if we had only been just a hair faster, we could have won the gold medal. Instead, he suggests we are better served to think like a bronze medalist — thrilled to be on the podium, happy and grateful because if we had been just a hair slower, chances are we would not have received any medal at all. [viii]

Failure in life is inevitable. The sooner we accept that fact and decide that we are going to see our failures as opportunities to learn, grow, and improve as we use them to our advantage, the better off we will be. When we fail, we need to ask ourselves what can we learn and do differently to secure a better outcome in the future, and then pick ourselves back up, dust ourselves off, and keep forging ahead.

Just as we need rain in order to get a rainbow, and if we get to appreciate the beauty of roses, we have to put up with their thorns, pursuing happiness doesn't come without its own set of costs. There will be failure and pain along the way. It simply isn't realistic to expect an obstacle-free journey through life.

If we want to experience the rewards that life has to offer, we have to be willing to accept the risks that come along for the ride. We have to let go of our quest for perfection, because perfection does not exist outside of our own minds and dreams. Everything brings with it its own problems and costs. It is when we let go of the notion of an arbitrary standard of perfection that we will find a great deal of stress lifted from our shoulders.

It is important to accept responsibility for fixing our own problems and be willing to push beyond our fears. We need to find our deep inner motivation and accept that there will be times in our lives when we are humiliated and experience failure, and then be brave enough to power through despite our fears as we strive for progress, rather than perfection.

Key Takeaways

- It is important to recognize our relationship with failure. If we allow a fear of failure to hold us back from fully participating in life, we will be preventing ourselves from discovering who we really are and growing to our full potential.
- We fail when we give in to our fear of failure and allow it to control our choices and actions, instead of accepting failure as a necessary learning opportunity in life and being willing to learn from our mistakes.
- We fail when we don't believe in ourselves enough to think we can find the solutions to any problem we need to overcome. We fail when we don't accept responsibility for our actions and problems and aren't willing to make the difficult choices to set ourselves apart.
- Getting to the true root of why we are afraid to fail is crucial if we are

going to be able to power through it and move beyond it.
- Happiness is never going to come without pain and failure. We need to find ways to use our failures to our advantage and learn from them in order to grow and improve.

Chapter 7: Living in the Age of More

Every parent wants to give their children more than they had growing up. Every parent wants a better life for their children than the one they had. However, every parent will tell you that as children receive more, their happiness usually doesn't increase. And if it does, it is very short-lived. Take my own children, for example: When they get a bunch of gifts all at once for their birthday or Christmas, they will often be a little overwhelmed and not know what to play with. In fact, they often revert back to playing with their old, familiar toys, or fuss and complain that their new ones are not performing the way they think they should. It is only when we get everything unpacked, organized, and put away where they can easily access it a little at a time that they begin to settle in with their new possessions.

How our world of more poisons us

Adults are really not that different from children, in that regard. Psychologists are perplexed at how over the past 50 years, with the standard of living increasing greatly in the civilized world, the levels of people's happiness have not shown the same increase we would expect. In fact, we are seeing increases in mental illness, depression, anxiety disorders, and narcissistic tendencies. [ix]

Our capitalist market may be contributing to this. It is a competitive market where businesses are constantly racing against one another for customers. Marketing 101 teaches students that fear sells. If businesses can convince people that their lives are inferior to others', they will be more likely to purchase goods to try to make themselves feel better about their life situation. While this is good for the businesses' bottom line, it isn't good for the human psyche, as people begin to internalize those feelings of inferiority or inadequacy.

Alain de Botton, a philosopher, wrote of this in his book *Status Anxiety*. He believes that in the past, people did not feel the stress they do today to advance their economic status. Long ago, people knew their standing in society. It was seen as a birthright and beyond a person's control. There was little opportunity for upward mobility, so people just accepted their status and went on about their lives without being consumed with getting ahead.

In today's society, there is much more pressure on the individual. People live in constant fear of losing the successes they have attained, or of not being good enough to advance their social status. They don't want to be seen as a failure or someone who wasted their opportunities and potential, and this causes an increase in anxiety. De Botton doesn't suggest that we need to return to the rigid social structures of the past, but he does point out that an increase in standard living and social mobility can also contribute to an increase in stress and anxiety. Welcome to the 21st century.

Today, we feel the need to be special

We have access to more information and people through the internet than we have before at any point in human history. While this can be amazingly positive, it also has the power to negatively impact our lives, at times. By having this unique perspective of the world, we may find ourselves constantly comparing ourselves to others and believing that the grass is always greener on the other side of the fence. We may never feel a sense of satisfaction with our lives as we scramble to try to keep up with everyone else. We may seek to change ourselves in order to distinguish ourselves from everyone else. This can result in:

- losing sight of who we really are and the things that bring meaning to our lives by trying to change ourselves to impress others;

- feeling like a failure if we don't feel we measure up;

- relying on the opinions of others, or a fleeting 15 minutes of fame to shape our self- image;

- or a sense of insignificance at the limits to our individual abilities to make a lasting impact affect change in a world filled with over 7.2 billion people.

According to Tony Robbins, all people have six human needs that drive everything we do:

1. Certainty — knowing you'll be able to avoid pain and feel pleasure.

2. Uncertainty/Variety — the need for change and new experiences.

3. Significance — feeling special and needed.

4. Connection/Love — feeling a close bond with others.

5. Growth — the ability to change and improve.

6. Contribution — the feeling that you are helping others and making a difference. [x]

He believes that each individual ranks these needs in their own unique order of importance. Robbins identifies the first four needs as those that shape our personalities, while the last two are our spiritual needs. He believes it is necessary to find a balance between these needs and to understand which are the biggest driving forces in our lives in order to achieve fulfillment. The two most troubling needs to give the most importance to are certainty (as it is impossible to avoid change in life) and significance (as it means you will always be at least subconsciously comparing yourself to others).

The bell curve of being special [xi]

The bell curve is a statistical analysis of where people fall in their performance. We typically think of the bell curve as being used to analyze test scores or IQ levels, but in reality, it holds true for the way people perform on nearly everything in life. 60% of people tend to perform at an average skill level, 20% of people tend to perform at an above-average skill level, and another 20% tend to perform below average. If you plot this on a graph, it will form a bell shape with a narrow point on each side representing the very small percentage of people who perform at a really outstanding level, or those that perform at an extremely low level.

Think of Lindsey Vonn, an extremely talented U.S. Olympic downhill skier, who performed at the highest levels of her sport for several years. She would definitely make up that very small top tier of athletes who can outperform nearly everyone else at the world championship and Olympic level, while I would make up the very small group of people who would perform at such a poor level that we would be ready to appear on a blooper reel. Her athletic abilities would likely have her performing at an average or above-average level of most sports, but she would probably not be able to perform at the highest pinnacle of any other sport, such as figure skating or hockey.

We all have limits. While it is important to try our best and not just sit back and be content to be mediocre at everything, it is also equally important to recognize that we all have strengths and weaknesses. We all have limits to our abilities, and try as we might, there will be some things that we aren't as good at as others. In fact, we will find ourselves falling in the average range of the bell curve more often than not, and that is okay, as long as we are giving our all. The reality is, at best, we can only hope to reach the very top tier of performers in only one area and only if we are lucky.

Think back to Lindsey Vonn. It took her years to hone her craft. Many, many hours of study and practice were needed to achieve her level of skill. Even if she wanted to, she couldn't reach that pinnacle of performance in multiple areas because there is simply not enough time in the day. Reaching the highest levels of performance takes a lot of time, energy, and effort, and it is simply impossible to devote those things to a multitude of areas which would require them.

The important thing is to discover who you really are and to get comfortable in your own skin — strengths, weaknesses, and all. Always strive for improvement, but realize there will be limits to what is possible and accept it as being okay. It is much better to be yourself than to just float around aimlessly, chasing whatever is trending on social media.

Is loneliness the result of "being special"?

As we discussed earlier, we live in a digital age that allows us to be connected to friends and family all over the world, courtesy of the internet. So why is it that several studies, including one conducted by Hazel Markus, a psychology professor at Stanford University, identify Americans, as well as those living in other western European countries, as being more lonely and having relatively few — if any — people with whom they can form deep connections with and trust opening up to about their problems?

It seems trite and easy to blame social media and texting or messaging others rather than meeting face to face to chat, but in reality, most people credit social media and today's technology with allowing them to feel more connected with their loved ones than ever before. So what causes this increased feeling of loneliness in some countries, but not in others?

It turns out that the countries in which people cite a greater feeling of loneliness are the very countries that place a high value on independence, uniqueness, and individualism. Think about it — from an early age, we start to ingrain these values in our children. We encourage them not to cry, to be "big girls and boys," and to rely more on themselves than others. We teach them to get up and brush themselves off when they are hurt, and to move on quickly from disappointments.

Don't get me wrong, these are important life skills to help our children, but they may be hearing our words in their heads years later as they enter adulthood, discouraging them from showing vulnerability to others and leaning on them in trying times. In our quest to stand out and be special, sometimes we can end up making ourselves feel isolated and lonely if we don't strike a sensible balance. It is important to bear in mind that one of our basic needs is to feel like we belong and to be connected with others. This has to be given equal value to attaining success. If we put all of our efforts into our work in order to get ahead, the feeling of loneliness will only deepen.

Key Takeaways:

- An increase in standard of living and material goods do not necessarily go hand in hand with an increased feeling of happiness. In fact, the opposite often seems to be true.

- Individuals feel greater pressure today than at any other point in human history to improve their social status, and this can be a source of anxiety and stress.

- Our desire to be special can cause us to lose sight of our true selves and what brings us meaning in our lives, if we try to change who we are in order to impress others.

- Despite our best efforts, the bell curve demonstrates that in most areas of our lives, we will fall within the average range of performance and ability.

- Our desire to be special, unique, and independent individuals can create a feeling of loneliness in our lives. We need to find a good balance between being independent and vulnerable.

Chapter 8: Find Your "Purpose"

Everyone wants to find their purpose in life. Looking for a deeper meaning and calling in life is a natural human tendency. It is a different journey for everyone. For some, it happens very quickly, while for others, it is a lengthy process that may take them in other directions first. Regardless of the path they take to get there, there is a commonality between all people in their quest to find their life's purpose. What they are essentially trying to find is how they can spend their time on something that is important. After all, the way we spend our days is the way we spend our lives.

My brothers both found their purpose in life in very different ways. One of my brothers always knew his life's work was to be a cardiologist. We lost our dad to a heart attack when I was just 14 years old. From that moment on, my brother knew he wanted to devote himself to saving others' lives so other families could be spared the pain and sadness that ours went through.

My other brother took a long time to figure out what he loved doing. He had always been passionate about coffee. In fact, I referred to him as a coffee snob on many occasions. It wasn't until he reached his early 40s that he decided to leave his career as a marketing manager in order to open up his own specialty coffee shop. Both of my brothers ultimately found their purpose, but they took very different paths to get there.

There are many things to consider as you try to decide what's important to you and how you will choose to spend your time. Some of them are:

- What are you willing to endure in the name of achieving your purpose?

When you find your purpose, you need to remember that things are not always going to be easy. No matter what you decide to pursue, there will be unpleasant aspects to contend with. There will be pain along with the joy and sacrifices you have to be willing to make. Whether it is spending long hours at work, spending years studying and honing your craft, being willing to take risks that frighten you, or countless other things, you will have to endure the bad in order to experience the good.

- What activities do you become so absorbed in that you lose track of time?

The things that consume your thoughts and energy in such a way that you don't think of anything else while you are engaged in them often provide you with clues that can lead you in the direction of your life's purpose.

- What scares you the most?

Human nature guides us to avoid what we are afraid of. No one wants to fail or humiliate themselves. Accomplishing great and important things requires us to go out on a limb and be willing to face our fears. It is the things that scare us most which should often be our life's purpose, because these are the things we give the most weight to in our lives.

- What is a problem in the world that you would most like to help solve, if you could?

We are given a finite amount of time to live our lives, so why not spend it making a difference? Start by volunteering your time trying to help solve a problem you feel passionately about. It just might lead you to your purpose, and even a different career path.

A good life isn't about finding your passion

Author and Georgetown University professor Cal Newport has ideas about how passion and work should be related. He believes that in general, people spend too much time thinking about what they want from their life instead of thinking about what skills and value they can bring to the table. He thinks it is possible to find joy in many different careers — we are not confined to only one path to one overriding passion in our lives. Newport stresses that it is less important to do what you love than it is to learn to love what you do. He claims that people experience greater satisfaction with their work when they feel like they have honed their craft and gained a level of expertise in their field. This enables them to feel a sense of control over, and become passionate about, their work. [xii]

There is no job in the world that you will honestly be able to say you enjoy every minute of. Even if you are in your absolute dream job, there will always be things that annoy you, times when you feel exhausted or overwhelmed, things that stress you out, and things you can complain about. That is simply a fact of life we must learn to accept. Having realistic expectations is key.

Looking for your purpose should not be a daunting task. Chances are it is right under your nose. How you spend your time when you have a choice and the issues you feel most passionate talking about are excellent places to begin your search.

Accept the bad with the good

Life is messy — not perfect. There will not be joy without pain or reward without sacrifice. These things go hand in hand in every area of our lives. This includes searching for our life's purpose. The quest to find a purpose and deeper meaning for one's life has greatly increased in popularity over the past few decades. People are no longer content to just have a successful career; they want to feel as if what they do is important and making a difference in the world.

The danger lies in people thinking that finding their purpose will solve all of their problems and guarantee them lifelong happiness. Little do they realize that it requires work and effort on their part and is not just a stroll through the park. They have unrealistic expectations that they will just suddenly know their purpose and be happy doing it for the rest of their lives. In reality, finding our purpose is a process of trial and error, and it is constantly evolving. The only guarantee we can bank on is that things will change, because we are always changing ourselves.

Even when we are doing what we love, we won't love every minute of what we do. There will be stressful situations and sources of frustration. There will be sacrifices we will have to make. Once you have found your purpose, you will be willing to stick with it even in the difficult times, accepting the bad in order to experience the good.

Key Takeaways:

- There is no one-size-fits-all method to finding your purpose and deeper meaning in life. It is a unique experience for everyone.

- Examining how you spend your time, issues you feel passionate about, activities that command your attention, and problems you would like to help solve are great places to start in your quest to find your purpose.

- It is possible to find purpose, meaning, and passion in many different areas and careers. Contemplating the skills and value you have to offer, and putting forth the time and effort necessary to hone your craft and achieve a level of expertise, will go a long way toward helping you learn to love what you do.

- Maintaining realistic expectations and recognizing that it is impossible to experience rewards without sacrifice are important to avoid disappointment as you search for your purpose in life.

- Finding your purpose is a process of trial and error that will evolve and change as you do.

Chapter 9: Be Grateful for What You Have Now

Be grateful for what you have now, for you will not truly appreciate what you have until it is gone. Parents can relate to how quickly their children grow. It seems that they progress through the stages and years of their childhood in the blink of an eye. With each passing birthday, parents often look back, wishing that they could keep their children that young for just a while longer.

Anyone who has lost someone they love understands what it is like to wish for just a few more days or hours with them. Being grateful for the time we have with loved ones and for the things we have in our lives makes us happier and allows us to appreciate the little things, which are really the important things, in life. Gratitude allows us to learn more about who we truly are and the things that we value the most. Being grateful for what we have simply makes us better people.

The benefits of gratitude

The human brain has a tendency to focus on the negative more than the positive. That means that being grateful might take a little extra practice and effort on our part. The happiest people are usually those who express gratitude and appreciation for what they have. Making the conscious choice to be present in the moment and practice gratitude will result in you experiencing an increased feeling of happiness.

Gratitude can increase our feelings of joy, compassion, peace, and awareness while making it more difficult to focus on feeling worry, loneliness, jealousy, and regret. Studies have shown that grateful people are more motivated and have a greater sense of purpose. They tend to experience less stress and greater satisfaction and happiness in their lives. They are more energetic, enthusiastic, and actively engaged in the world around them.

Scientific research has backed this up time after time. A 2014 study published in *Emotion* found that expressing gratitude can lead to new relationships and opportunities by creating a feeling of goodwill that others will want to continue.

A 2012 study published in *Personality and Individual Differences* found that people who are grateful are more likely to take good care of their health. They tend to exercise more often and visit their doctors for regular checkups, which contributes to their better overall health. Researcher Robert Emmons has conducted multiple studies that have found grateful people tend to experience greater feelings of happiness and less depression. [xiii]

The University of Kentucky conducted a study in 2012 which found that grateful people are usually more sensitive and compassionate toward others and less likely to seek revenge for perceived wrongdoings. They come across as just being nicer human beings in general.

Multiple studies have found a connection between gratitude and increased mental strength and resiliency, even in the most difficult of times. A 2006 study published in *Behavior Research and Therapy* found that Vietnam War veterans who expressed more gratitude experienced fewer symptoms of post-traumatic stress disorder. The *Journal of Personality and Social Psychology* published a 2003 study which found that those who experienced the devastating September 11th terrorist attacks were likely to have a stronger and more lasting recovery if gratitude played a prominent role in their lives. [xiv]

One of the world's leading authorities on gratitude, Dr. Robert Emmons, a professor of psychology at the University of California, Davis, has conducted several studies which may have implications for how you can immediately start practicing a little more gratitude in your life. In a 2003 study, Emmons and a professor from the University of Miami, Michael McCullough, collaborated to assess the effects of writing in a gratitude journal on approximately 200 college students. The participants in the study were divided into three groups, which were asked to write journal entries for 10 weeks. One group wrote about things they were grateful for, one group wrote about stresses in their lives, and one group wrote about neutral events. After 10 weeks, the group who wrote about the things they were grateful for said that they felt more positive and optimistic about their lives and felt better physically. The researchers were surprised that there was not more of an improvement in overall mood noted. [xv]

They wondered if writing in the gratitude journal more than once a week would make a difference, so they conducted another study. This time, the participants were asked to write in their journals every day for two weeks. There were still three groups asked to write on the same topics as in the first study, except the group that had previously been asked to write about neutral events was now tasked with writing about ways in which they felt as though they were better off than others. The results of this study indicated that the participants who had written about the things they were grateful for reported being in a better mood during the study's time frame, but this time, they didn't say that they were feeling any health benefits as the group in the previous study had.

Now the researchers predicted that two weeks was not enough time for health benefits to kick in, so they decided to conduct a third study. In this study, 65 adult participants who suffered from neuromuscular disease were split into two groups. One group was asked to write about the things they were grateful for, while the other group just filled out a questionnaire assessing their overall mood and health. Both groups were asked to participate for three weeks. At the end of the study, the group that had written in their gratitude journals said that they felt more positive about their lives, were in a better mood during the study, and felt better physically because they were able to get more quality sleep than those who did not. These results were also confirmed by their partners.

These three studies indicate that consistently writing in a gratitude journal for even a short time each day can lead to improved physical, mental, and emotional health. [xvi]

Simple ways to practice gratitude

Now that we have discovered some of the benefits being grateful can have on us, like a stronger immune system, increased feelings of happiness and optimism, and reduced feelings of loneliness and sadness, let's focus on some easy ways we can practice gratitude in our daily lives.

It is not necessary to devote a lot of time to practicing being grateful, but it is helpful to make a consistent and conscious commitment to expressing gratitude every day in order to gain the most benefits from it. This can be achieved by making some very simple additions to your daily routine. You might just find that you will discover more about yourself and what's truly important to you in the process, and perhaps even become a better person along the way.

- Write in a gratitude journal each day.
- Be present in the moment and be grateful for what you have now.
- Find ways to help those who are less fortunate than you. You will really start to appreciate everything you have.
- Make sure to take every opportunity you can to let your loved ones know how much you appreciate them and are grateful to have them in your life.

The human brain has a natural tendency to focus on the negative — the things we don't have and the things that are going wrong. Practicing gratitude does not allow us to dwell on the negative because it makes us stay focused on the present moment — the things we do have, the things in our lives that are going well, and the positive gifts we have been given. When we focus on the good, there simply no time to dwell on the bad. Our whole outlook and attitude changes, and we feel much more at peace with our place in the world.

Key Takeaways:

- Practicing gratitude allows us to learn more about ourselves and the things we truly value in our lives.
- Practicing gratitude takes a conscious effort on our part. Our brain has a tendency to focus on the negative rather than the positive, so this paradigm shift is not one that comes easily or naturally. It will take time to improve our expression of gratitude until it becomes second nature to us.
- When we practice gratitude, we feel happier, healthier, and have a greater sense of purpose in our lives.

- Many scientific studies back up the benefits we receive from expressing gratitude.
- It is possible to do little things each day to focus on the things we are grateful for and reap the benefits from it.

Chapter 10: Lessons Learned: What Would I Tell My Teenaged, 20-, 30-, and 40-year-old Self?

You always hear people say, "Oh, if I could only be (some age) again and know then what I know now..." Well, now that I have reached the wise and mature age of 50, I am reflecting upon the wisdom I would like to share with my teenaged, 20-, 30-, and 40-year-old self.

Teens

- Your parents are not trying to ruin your life, no matter how it seems. Your mother is not a bad person — she is a single mother doing her best to keep up with her three sons. She doesn't make you do chores and mow the lawn because she wants to sabotage your Saturday night plans. She is exhausted and needs help at home, since your two brothers are working while they are also going to college. Which takes me to the next point: your brother doesn't want to make you feel inferior or a loser — he is older and, unlike you at the moment, has a purpose in life.

- Parents are just human beings who love you very much and want what they think is best for you. They have been down the road you're traveling, and they want to keep you from making the same mistakes or experiencing some of the heartbreak they did. Try to go easy on them. One day, you will appreciate everything they have done for you.
- You may think you will never get over some of the bad things that will happen soon, but they really are not the end of the world, I promise. One day, you'll look back and they won't even be a blip on your radar.

- Exercise, get your sleep, and try to eat a little healthier. One day, these choices will catch up with you, and you'll be glad you did.
- Try not to worry so much about being popular. Most of your high school peers will not be your lifelong friends. Focus more on being true to yourself and doing what you know in your heart is right. Ultimately, the kids will respect you for it.
- You care about people and love teaching — embrace it. It is not lame; it is what you can do best. Otherwise, be patient with yourself. You are a work in progress, and you don't need to try to figure everything out right now.
- College will help you become more social and will open your eyes to the fact that often, your best friends are books.
- Invest in the internet business in the '90s. Seriously.

20s

- You've spent your whole life so far trying to get older faster. Now it's time to slow things down and just enjoy the ride. Take things as they come. There is no rush.
- Don't let your new responsibilities frighten and intimidate you. You were raised well, and you have plenty of people who love you and are happy to help if they can. Don't hesitate to reach out to them for guidance as you learn more about who you are and try to find your way.
- Don't let a fear of failure keep you from living your life to the fullest. Step out of your comfort zone to travel to new places, meet new people, and try new things. Fail now, and fail big. This is the right time to do it. This is the time to make mistakes, run away with some girl just to realize in three weeks that you're a horrible match, start a business and fail, or change colleges, because this is the time when you're not a kid anymore, but you aren't responsible for other adult

things like a wife, kids, or a mortgage. It is good to exercise some caution and be responsible, but it is also okay to make a few mistakes along the way. That is often when you learn your biggest and most important lessons.

- Cherish your memories and childhood friendships, but don't hold onto them so tightly that you miss out on all of the exciting new adventures that await you and the wonderful new friends you are about to make. It is natural to grow apart a bit after high school. The friends who are meant to be with you for the long haul will find their way back into your life again in the future.
- The universe doesn't owe you the courtesy of making sense. Not everything will, and certainly not in the moment when you wish it would. Try to understand that everything happens for a reason, and while it may not suit your current time frame or make sense to you right now, one day, it will.

- Be grateful for all the people who love you and who have made sacrifices in their lives that helped to shape you into the person you are today. You are lucky to be blessed with such amazing people in your life who are so invested in you and your happiness.
- Be less arrogant. Being at the top of your class in college won't matter if you sabotage it with your attitude.
- You won't get everything you want — especially not all at once. You will get there. You'll study biology. You'll be a teacher. You'll coach people. You'll write books… by the time you're 50. You won't accomplish all of that in your 20s, and that's okay.
- People are not so different in the world. They mostly share the same fears, problems, and things that make them happy — you can connect with many more people than you think. And you will. At the end of the day, what someone likes and dislikes defines a person.

- Nope, no one cares that much about you — whether you gained three pounds, whether you got an F, whether you didn't show up for a party. You are not that important; sorry to break it down to you. Just think about how much time you spend on thinking about others versus yourself.
- Finishing as a top student won't give you as much as you think. Winning the running competition won't give you what you think. Life's joy is in the collection of small things, not the big milestones.
- Your mom really did the best she could. Without her hard work and sacrifice, you wouldn't have made to college or have any prospects in life. Of course, she was overwhelmed and impatient from time to time, but that's only human. The true path to adulthood is to stop blaming your parents and find reason, acceptance, and forgiveness toward them.

30s

- It is important to be financially responsible. Seek advice from others who are knowledgeable and start saving money for a rainy day, as well as your future. You will want to buy a house, have a family, be financially secure, and retire comfortably one day. It isn't too early to set money aside for all of these things.
- Be conscious of the choices you are making today that will impact your health down the road. Exercise, eat healthier, go for your checkups, and take care of yourself. You will be happy you did.
- Try not to be too hard on yourself. You really did turn out okay, and you are still a work in progress. You will have an amazing life complete with many dreams come true — some of which you didn't even know you had.
- Give back to your community and try to make the world a better place for your children. You have talents that will prove

beneficial and a heart for helping others. Don't waste them.
- Make a commitment to spend as much time as possible with your parents, spouse, and children. If you don't, you will miss out on so much that you can't get back. One day, your children will be grown and your mom will be gone. Spending time with them making memories will be the best investment you will ever make. Time is precious, and you won't regret a single second.
- Be present when you are with your family. Your 30s are the years when your parents will make more sense to you, and you can understand and know them more as adults.
- Be good and generous with those who are good and generous with you. Eliminate people who drag you down or hold you back.
- If you don't have all figured out, that's good too. If you feel at the age of 35 that you need to make a career change, allow yourself the risk. You're not too late.

Don't stick to something to look like an adult who is "ready," just to regret it later… in your 40s and 50s.

- Learning doesn't stop at school, especially when you have so much access to knowledge. As Warren Buffett once said, "The greatest investment a young person can make is in their own education, in their own mind. Because money comes and goes. Relationships come and go. But what you learn once stays with you forever."
- Start treating yourself better. You are not in the awkward teenage years and you know you are human, just like everybody else. Embrace it. Embrace who you are and love yourself.

40s

- Don't postpone anything. Keep active and moving at every opportunity. I feel the 40s are our last call to start to work on a long-cherished dream with faith that you'll be able to reach it. Some people can do it later, but with much more effort — and let's face it, we don't like too much effort at that age.

- Eat healthier than in your 30s and take care of yourself. Its time to give some credit to Whole Foods and spend more on your health — vitamins, fruits, veggies, and better quality of food overall. You want to be around for a long, long time so that you can experience all of the joys life has to offer.
- Invest more time and money in sports. Always wanted to play squash or golf, but it seemed snobbish and overrated? Well, hopefully not anymore. Realize that at the age of 40, nothing is lame anymore. Embrace it. Explore new hobbies and take the vacations you always wanted to. Stop putting things off and enjoy every moment.
- Start thinking of the legacy you will leave behind.
- Realize that age is just a number and try not to let it affect your state of mind. Keep approaching things in life with the

same sense of wonder and joy that you did as a child. Try to look at life through the eyes of your children. Live life to the fullest and be comfortable in your own skin.

- Share memories with family and friends. Look back on them with fondness and have a good laugh at how seriously you used to take the insignificant stuff.
- Find humor in your life. Never stop having fun! Contemplate on the good, the bad, and the ugly of your past decades and realize that with time, all of them faded, and find some humor in how fatalistically you've approached some stuff when you were younger. Don't get so hung up on making a living that you forget to take time to enjoy your life.
- Don't lose your inner child. By the time you're 40, you pretty much have seen it all — you experienced wonder and loss, and hopefully you've traveled. You've worked, gotten fired, made your fortune, had a child, lost a parent or grandparent. Some of my fellow dad friends often say,

"Nothing can surprise me anymore." No, don't let yourself burn out to that level. Let everyday wonders capture you as they did when you first discovered them. Go and re-explore things with your children and relive first time wonders through their eyes. Enjoy the sunshine and dance in the rain. You are alive and you are young.

There is no such thing as true perfection — only perfect progression. There is always room to grow and improve at every age. Embrace it and always try to be your very best self. Then it will truly be a wonderful life.

Key Takeaways:

- We are truly works in progress, no matter what age we are.
- There is no such thing as true perfection. We always have room to grow and improve.

- We do what we can with what we have where we are, and when we know better, we do better.
- Since we do not have the benefit of hindsight when things are happening in our lives, we should just try to take things in stride. As long as we are trying our best, we are doing okay, and we shouldn't be overly hard on ourselves. We can take some comfort in knowing that things are rarely as bad as they seem in the moment.
- Never let the fear of failure prevent you from living your life to the fullest.

Closing

As we go on the journey of trying to find who we are meant to be and fulfill our life's purpose, we must keep in mind that we are works in progress who are always growing and changing. All too often, we give our power away to others. We rely too heavily on specific people, or even things, thinking that they are the keys to our happiness. In reality, we make our own happiness. Being grateful for the things we have now instead of always being focused on what we don't have and wanting more will carry us a long way toward that happiness.

We live in fear that the people and things that are meeting our needs today will be gone tomorrow. This is entirely possible, as most people and things come and go, with very few of them being permanent fixtures in our lives. But what we fail to realize is that in most cases, we are perfectly capable of withstanding their departure and, in time, being just fine.

We mistakenly think we need our current romantic partner, when in reality, we need to be loved. We think we need our present job, when we really just need stable employment to ensure our financial security. We try to hold on to these specific people and things at all costs to ensure our happiness.

The only thing constant in our lives is change. It is inevitable. We won't be able to protect ourselves from ever feeling sadness or loss. This is simply unrealistic. But our happiness isn't dependent upon us never suffering a loss in our lives. It is dependent on how we respond to the losses we do sustain. If we take the lessons we learn from them, we can use them to our advantage and create a brighter future for ourselves than we ever imagined.

It is not easy to accept the losses of the people and things we hold dear, but it is possible. When we realize we are the architects of our own happiness, we come to understand that even if we lose "everything," as long as we have ourselves, we can mourn the losses, pick ourselves up, dust ourselves off, and begin anew, finding people and things that meet our needs and add meaning to our lives.

We can't let the fear of failure dictate our lives and keep us from living them to the fullest. We must always do our best, but in reality, even then we will only be performing at an average skill level in most areas. Accepting this will help to alleviate the pressure of feeling that we need to be special and unique in every circumstance, as well as the feelings of loneliness and isolation that often go along with it.

We can never lose sight of the fact that we can't have reward without sacrifice or joy without pain. Figuring out what we are willing to endure in our quest for happiness and fulfillment is a key part of knowing ourselves.

Self-discovery is a journey that is never truly complete. There is an old Quaker saying, "Let your life speak," that would serve well as a guiding life principle. The more we learn about ourselves, the more likely we will be to find our purpose and a deeper meaning in our lives. We will be able to stay true to ourselves and not just trade in our core values for the latest fads and trends. And that will be a life well-lived, indeed.

The best of luck on your journey!

Steven

Reference

Anxiety And Depression Association of America. Facts and Statistics. Anxiety And Depression Association of America. 2018.
https://adaa.org/about-adaa/press-room/facts-statistics

Bergman, Peter. Diversify Your Self. Harvard Business Review. 2009.
https://hbr.org/2009/10/diversify-yourself

Das, Subhamoy. The 4 Stages of Life in Hinduism. Thought Co. 2017.
https://www.thoughtco.com/stages-of-life-in-hinduism-1770068

Fearon, James D. What Is Identity (As We Now Use The Word)? Stanford University. 1999.
https://web.stanford.edu/group/fearon-

research/cgi-bin/wordpress/wp-content/uploads/2013/10/What-is-Identity-as-we-now-use-the-word-.pdf

Goldberg, Lynne. The Secret to Happiness: 5 Tips to Feel More Grateful and Blissful. Tiny Buddha. 2018. https://tinybuddha.com/blog/secret-happiness-5-tips-feel-grateful-blissful/

Greenberg, Melanie. PhD. How Gratitude Leads to a Happier Life. Psychology Today. 2015. https://www.psychologytoday.com/us/blog/the-mindful-self-express/201511/how-gratitude-leads-happier-life

Lawrence, Tracy. The Life Portfolio: Diversify Your Identity to Maximize Your Life. Be Yourself. 2015. https://byrslf.co/the-life-portfolio-diversify-your-identity-to-maximize-your-life-41a6b475e061

Mapes, James J., Quantum Leap Thinking: An Owner's Guide to the Mind. Sourcebooks. 2003.

Manson, Mark. In Defense of Being Average. Mark Manson. 2015.
https://markmanson.net/being-average

Morin, Amy. 7 Scientifically Proven Benefits of Gratitude. Psychology Today. 2015.
https://www.psychologytoday.com/us/blog/what-mentally-strong-people-dont-do/201504/7-scientifically-proven-benefits-gratitude

Mueller, Steven. The Four Stages of Life. Planet of Success. 2017.
http://www.planetofsuccess.com/blog/2016/the-four-stages-of-life/

Newport, Cal. So Good They Can't Ignore You. Piatkus. 2016.

Sivers, Derek. Think like a bronze medalist, not silver. Derek Sivers. 2017.
https://sivers.org/bronze

Team Tony. Do You Need To Feel Significant? Tony Robbins. 2018.
https://www.tonyrobbins.com/mind-meaning/do-you-need-to-feel-significant/

Endnotes

---

[i] Das, Subhamoy. The 4 Stages of Life in Hinduism. Thought Co. 2017.
https://www.thoughtco.com/stages-of-life-in-hinduism-1770068

[ii] Mueller, Steven. The Four Stages of Life. Planet of Success. 2017.
http://www.planetofsuccess.com/blog/2016/the-four-stages-of-life/

[iii] Mueller, Steven. The Four Stages of Life. Planet of Success. 2017.
http://www.planetofsuccess.com/blog/2016/the-four-stages-of-life/

[iv] Bergman, Peter. Diversify Your Self. Harvard Business Review. 2009.
https://hbr.org/2009/10/diversify-yourself

[v] Fearon, James D. What Is Identity (As We Now Use The Word)? Stanford University. 1999. https://web.stanford.edu/group/fearon-research/cgi-bin/wordpress/wp-content/uploads/2013/10/What-is-Identity-As-we-now-use-the-word-.pdf

[vi] Lawrence, Tracy. The Life Portfolio: Diversify Your Identity to Maximize Your Life. Be Yourself. 2015. https://byrslf.co/the-life-portfolio-diversify-your-identity-to-maximize-your-life-41a6b475e061

[vii] Mapes, James J., Quantum Leap Thinking: An Owner's Guide to the Mind. Sourcebooks. 2003.

[viii] Sivers, Derek. Think like a bronze medalist, not silver. Derek Sivers. 2017. https://sivers.org/bronze

[ix] Anxiety And Depression Association of America. Facts and Statistics. Anxiety And Depression Association of America. 2018. https://adaa.org/about-adaa/press-room/facts-statistics

[x] Team Tony. Do You Need To Feel Significant? Tony Robbins. 2018. https://www.tonyrobbins.com/mind-meaning/do-you-need-to-feel-significant/

[xi] Manson, Mark. In Defense of Being Average. Mark Manson. 2015. https://markmanson.net/being-average

[xii] Newport, Cal. So Good They Can't Ignore You. Piatkus. 2016.

[xiii] Morin, Amy. 7 Scientifically Proven Benefits of Gratitude. Psychology Today. 2015. https://www.psychologytoday.com/us/blog/what-mentally-strong-people-dont-

do/201504/7-scientifically-proven-benefits-gratitude

[xiv] Morin, Amy. 7 Scientifically Proven Benefits of Gratitude. Psychology Today. 2015. https://www.psychologytoday.com/us/blog/what-mentally-strong-people-dont-do/201504/7-scientifically-proven-benefits-gratitude

[xv] Greenberg, Melanie. PhD. How Gratitude Leads to a Happier Life. Psychology Today. 2015. https://www.psychologytoday.com/us/blog/the-mindful-self-express/201511/how-gratitude-leads-happier-life

[xvi] Goldberg, Lynne. The Secret to Happiness: 5 Tips to Feel More Grateful and Blissful. Tiny Buddha. 2018. https://tinybuddha.com/blog/secret-happiness-5-tips-feel-grateful-blissful/

www.ingramcontent.com/pod-product-compliance
Lightning Source LLC
Chambersburg PA
CBHW052042280426
43661CB00085B/46